Natural Rhythms of Main Beach Queensland

John Tilston

i

John Tilston
Serisier Avenue
Main Beach
Queensland
Australia
www.johntilston.com

Table of contents

To Rosemary, who explored all with me and fell in love with the family of black swans along the way

Main Beach Queensland

Is there anyone who can watch without fascination the struggle for supremacy between sea and land?

The sea attacks relentlessly, marshalling the force of its powerful waves against the land's strongest points. It collects the energy of distant winds and transports it across thousands of miles of open ocean as quietly as rolling swell. On nearing shore this calm disguise is suddenly cast off, and the waves rise up as angry breakers, hurling themselves against the land in a final furious assault. Turbulent water, green and white, is flung against sea cliffs and forced into cracks between the rocks to dislodge them. When pieces fall, the churning water grinds them against each other to form sand; the sand already on the beach melts away before the onslaught.

But the land defends itself with such subtle skill that often it will gain ground in the face of the attack. Sometimes it will trade a narrow zone of high cliff for a whole low beach. Or it may use some of its beach material in a flanking manoeuvre to seal off the arms of the sea that have recklessly reached between the headlands. The land constantly straightens its front to present the least possible shoreline to the sea's onslaught.

When the great storm waves come, the beach will temporarily retreat, slyly deploying part of its material in a sandy underwater bar that forces the waves to break prematurely and spend their energies in futile foam and turbulence before they reach the main coast. When the storm subsides, the small waves that follow contritely return the sand to widen the beach again. Rarely can either of the antagonists claim a permanent victory.

extract from *Waves and Beaches: The powerful dynamics of Sea and Coast* by William Bosom and Kim McCoy

On the beach

Early mornings on the beaches of Main Beach, weather permitting, remind you that you are in a little piece of paradise. The sun rises over the Pacific, brilliantly colouring the world emerging from the total darkness that is the sea at night. These early mornings are tranquil, inspiring you to contemplate life or the trials of day ahead with calmness and composure. By afternoon, the heat may have set in and the onshore breeze will be blowing, making you less at peace and more inclined to laugh out loud at the joy of life on a beach. Either way, it is a privilege to be so close and intimate with a primal force of nature.

And primal it is here at Main Beach. If you go further south on this unbroken stretch of 16 kilometres of beach, towards Surfers Paradise your sense of the natural environment can be overshadowed, quite literally, by the high rises along the Esplanade. But just north of the Main Beach high rise apartment blocks, beyond the Southport Surf Club, the beach is buttressed by trees. You are on a beach isolated from urban sprawl. It is a delicious irony. You can be within 200 metres of surely one of the most densely developed suburbs in Australia and yet feel as though you are on an island.

There are other ironies too. This bushland along the beach is not a remnant passed over by, or a survivor of urban development. No. It is man made too, but man-made in keeping with what was here before.

As a relative newcomer this has made me want to dig a little deeper; to understand more about nature here at Main Beach. It is the natural environment - its nature - that makes it special, despite an array of fine restaurants and other man-made entertainments.

When you feel the fine golden sand on the glorious stretches of Main Beach between your toes you might care to ponder that it hasn't been there very long. Like so many of our visitors, it has come from down south. On beaches where the waves hit the shore square on, much sand stays in place. But along the east coast of Australia, the prevailing surf comes from the south east, hitting most beaches at an angle, pushing, pulling and dragging sand ever northwards, until halted by man-made sea walls, like the seawall at the Spit at the northern extremity of Main Beach. The natural shifting of this sand is known as Longshore drift.

Regular erosion

Marine specialists have calculated that an average of about 500,000 cubic metres - about eight million tonnes - moves northward across Gold Coast beaches each year, though the actual volume each year varies a great deal depending on the how often strong south easterly winds batter the coast. This is a lot of sand. Imagine a three story building, ten metes wide, stretching all the way from the Spit seawall to Narrowneck, and you get an idea of just how much it is.

The soft sand on the beach is almost-pure quartz with an average grain size of a quarter of a millimetre. Over millennia the sand has eroded from extensive granite rocks in the New England Highlands of New South Wales and delivered to the coast by northern New South Wales rivers: the Hastings, Macleay, Richmond, Clarence, Brunswick and the Tweed. Once at the river mouths the sand is transported north by waves. Some of it comes from as far south as Port Macquarie, a journey of some 800 kilometres. Geologists reckon that much of the sand transfer probably occurred when the sea was at a lower level, when there were fewer headlands that now compartmentalise the east coast and interrupt the movement. Still, the 500,000 cubic metres does cross the border at the Tweed River seawall onto Gold Coast beaches courtesy of a sand pumping system operated cooperatively by both state governments.

Over the millennia, the Longshore drift has created the world's largest accumulation of sand in south east Queensland's six sand islands: Fraser (soon to be known by its First Nation people's place name K'gari - pronounced Gurri), Cooloola, Bribie, Moreton (Mulgumpin), North Stradbroke (Minjerribah) and South Stradbroke, the latter just across the seaway at the Spit (and known to local surfers as TOS - The Other Side of the seaway). The six islands together are made up of about 250 cubic kilometres of sand, suggesting that at today's rate of sand flow, it took about 500,000 years for them to reach their present size They are estimated to date back about two million years, which is not much more than the blink of an eye in geological terms.

Though not directly relevant for Main Beachers, today the final terminus for the ever north moving sand is the 30 kilometre long Breaksea Spit, at the northern tip of Fraser Island (K'gari). The island and natural spit have extended so far across to the continental shelf that the sand moves along the spit to the edge of the shelf, then cascades into the deep ocean beyond.

And before our direct intervention, especially at the Spit, the longshore drift caused the mouth of the Nerang River to incrementally move north. Over time the river mouth moved northward by up to 60 metres each year, which is quite a lot when you think about it, causing land erosion and changing sandbanks at the bar and adjoining Broadwater. In the early 1800s the Nerang River entered the Ocean opposite where the Star Gold Coast casino at Broadbeach is now. In 1930 the entrance was opposite where Seaworld is today.

In 1986 the natural movement of the sand further north was halted and the Nerang River mouth permanently fixed in place by the construction of the seawall at the Spit. It was an epic project costing $50 million that deposited one million tonnes of imported rock, two layers of 20 and 25 tonne concrete cubes (4,500 cubes in total) and dredged 4.5 million cubic metres of sand. But so as to not denude South Stradbroke and deny other northern beaches of their migrating sand, a large-capacity fixed-sand bypassing system was built. It consists of a 500-metre-long jetty located about 250 metres south of the southern training wall. It pumps hundreds of thousands of cubic metres of sand across the Seaway each year, depending on the weather conditions.

The seawall breakwaters are at an angle of 15 degrees north of east to reduce the direct entry of ocean swells into the Broadwater. It was also deemed necessary to build an island - aptly called

Wavebreak Island, it does what it says on the tin - to capture storm waves and protect the western foreshore of the Broadwater.

Recently, the Gold Coast City Council has decided to redirect some of the sand from the Spit's sand bypassing system to the south. At the time of writing, it is installing a 7.8 kilometre pipeline that will deliver sand from the Spit to the northern beaches to offset coastal erosion. Once completed, 6.3 kilometres of permanent pipe will run underground and connect to 1.5 kilometres of temporary above-ground pipe to funnel the sand to Surfers Paradise and Main Beach. The pipeline has the capacity to redirect up to 20 per cent or around 120,000 cubic metres of the sand, almost 200,000 tonnes, south each year.

The Main Beach coastline, as with others north and south, has been constantly moving. It has moved quite dramatically even over the last 200,000 years, which is less than the blink of an eye in geological time. Long before man-induced climate change became a serious challenge in our times, there have been fluctuations in the sea level, caused by natural variations in the Earth's climate. In the Ice Ages the polar caps expanded, drawing water from the oceans and lowering sea levels. At such times, the coast line of the whole Gold Coast was up to 150 metres lower than now, and about 40 kilometres east of the present shoreline. In warmer times, the sea rose and pushed westward. We are now in a warmer phase of the Earth's natural climate cycle, even without accounting for warming effects of man-made climate change, compared with average conditions over the past million years. So our present sea level at Main Beach is near the highest over that time. Geologists say is was slightly higher about 7000 years ago, after the sea rose at the end of the last Ice Age, then it settled and stabilised at its present level and position about 6000 years ago.

The Beach faces almost due east, wonderful viewing for sunrises, and is hit by a predominantly southerly swell averaging 1.5 metres. This has combined with the generally fine sand to

Courtesy of Gold Coast City Council

produce a wide, low gradient high tide beach fronted by a 150 to 200 metre wide surf zone containing two sand bars. It is a wonderful beach to walk along. The inner bar is usually just beyond the water's edge and, depending on wave conditions, may be continuous with a few rips (rips are narrow channels of fast moving water returning to the ocean - more of that later) or, during and following higher waves, cut by deep rip channels every 200 to 250 metres along the beach. There is a continuous deep trough that runs parallel to this inner bar further into the water that is cut by more widely spaced rips. There are permanent rips at the northern end of the beach on the southern side of the Nerang mouth seawall and at the sand bypassing jetty just to the south. Deep holes and permanent rips run out by the wall, while there are strong currents in the inlet.

* * *

If you were to look at the Main Beach sand through a microscope, you would see many different rocks, gemstones and shells. It takes many years for a rock to break down to the size of a grain. The motion of waves, wind and currents makes sure that the sand moves along the coast and becomes finer in the process. The softer rocks are worn away the fastest, exposing the jade, quartz and sometimes even gold, or so it is alleged.

Main Beach and the Gold Coast beaches generally are very fortunate to have fine, golden sand. There are many beaches in the world where pebbles or gritty sand make up the coastline. The Coast's high-energy waves, which have relatively long wavelengths, produce a beach surface where the size of each sand grain is roughly the same as any other. Lower energy waves, which have smaller wavelengths, tend to produce beach surfaces with a more mixed grain sizes. The gentle slope of our beaches also helps create the fine sand. A steeper beach would generate larger grain size because bigger particles can be cast higher up the beach by the waves on steep beaches. On flatter beaches, like ours, sand grains tend to be rolled back and forth and broken into smaller pieces.

There are around eight billion grains of sand per cubic metre of beach. so you can imagine, sort of, how many grains of sand there are on Main Beach. Yet every grain of sand is microscopically unique.

On the beach, we usually see seagulls, sometimes catch sight of whales close in and see people fishing pulling in a fish. If we are patient, we might also see a crab or two. But otherwise the beach appears barren and not likely to be a place for life of any sort to thrive. Yet the sand and surf host an entire world of microscopic plankton that lives in the water, and microscopic animals and algae that live in the space between the sand grains. The sand and space between grains receive good penetration from sunlight providing energy for this microscopic life. Most are also exposed to constant water movement. which has the potential to circulate nutrients and exchange water and nutrients with the coastal ocean, inlets and streams. It can also be a little rough, so the beach only works for specially adapted life. These minute organisms live both on the sand and between the grains. The empty spaces between the grains can be as much as 40 per cent of the beach volume. And smaller sand grains offer much more surface area than larger ones in any given spot. These surfaces host microscopic bacteria, fungi, and small single-cell algae called diatoms.

The sand also hosts what are called meiofauna. Marine meiofauna are typically tiny, ranging between 32 microns (32/1000 of a millimetre, which is too small to be seen by the naked human eye) and up to one millimetre in size. These are minute animals that include a wonderfully diverse and important, yet often overlooked, part of marine ecosystems. They are extremely small worms and several types of shrimp; single cell organisms that come in many shapes and sizes (known as protozoa). They are usually worm-shaped to enable them to move easily through the sand grains. There could be up to one million of these little creatures in each square metre. But oddly, or at least we don't yet know why, many of these tiny creatures are gregarious. Species tend to hang out together and form patchy clusters along the shore.

But sandy beaches like the ones at Main Beach, are a tough environment to survive in. There is high physical stress of waves pounding in and continued churn of the sand, while the intertidal area is alternatively submerged and exposed. Consequently, these little beach critters are what scientists call 'impoverished', meaning they don't get fat or too comfortable. One of their common characteristics is great mobility and usually the ability to burrow rapidly. This is especially the case on Main Beach, which is dominated by waves delivering the most harsh intertidal climates: the more mobile the tiny animal, the faster it can burrow and the more likely it is to survive through the tough physical forces operating at the beach face. Marine biologists have not discovered any that stay in one place.

Given the relentless, turbulent life they lead, these beach creatures tend to eat whatever they can get. Few specialise in one type of food, some species feed in more than one way depending on what sort of food is available at any given time. Because of the highly erratic food supply, many species are capable of scavenging and filter-feeding, which enables them to eat the more constant tiny chunks of debris of all sorts; bacteria and dissolved organic matter which is percolated through the sand from the sea. Many meiofauna move through the sediment, secrete trails of mucus, and can stimulate growth of bacteria, which helps with moving nutrients and stabilising the sediment grains, keeping them stuck together and helping to avoid erosion by tides and waves. Living beneath the sand surface, many beach animals have reduced eyes or eyes positioned on the end of slender stalks. They are a food sources for small fish, large worms, and crabs that sift through sediments, for instance. Several intertidal beach species have the ability to regrow limbs or other body extremities hacked off by predators. This is particularly useful when they escape an attack by fish and birds but are wounded.

* * *

Of course, you can't walk along Main Beach these days and not be struck by the erosion evident by the 2.5 metre high banks 20 metres or so from the waters' edge at low tide to realise what a tough life it must be for the sand creatures. But it also reminds you of the immense amount of sand that is moved, especially during the storms. Not too long ago, a private residence on the beach at Woodroffe Avenue rather optimistically, or perhaps naively, erected a wooden pole and wire mesh fence at the property's eastern boundary on the edge of the sand bank. One or two days of heavy storms effectively washed the fence away by gouging out the sand bank and exposing and undermining the concrete bases sunk into the sand to supposedly secure the fence poles. This was the cause of much merriment from the locals, some of whom had already objected to a new brick wall built at right angles to the fence and partially obscuring the view north along the beach from the viewing platform at the end of Woodroffe Avenue.

The Gold Coast City Council says it's important to have a certified seawall in place to protect your property from this sort of eventuality and it is a condition before planning approval is granted, so one hopes the house with the dodgy fence has one buried perhaps closer in. This general protection - put in place by the Council on public land and by private owners on their land - takes the form of a boulder seawall buried out of sight beneath sand dunes along what is called the A line. The A line and other protective measures were introduced after a rough period in the 1960s and early 1970s.

The Gold Coast had particularly severe beach erosion in 1967, when five tropical cyclones and three severe East Coast lows hit

Damage done in 1967 storms

within six months; Tropical Cyclone Dinah was at the time considered a 1-in-100 year event, with a surge of 1.5 metres. Experts at Griffith University reckon that year was the biggest single combination of events causing beach erosion in our known history of the Gold Coast. There was no time for beaches to recover between the cataclysmic storms. An estimated eight million cubic metres of sand - sixteen times the average yearly longshore drift - was removed from Gold Coast beaches in the first half of 1967. Half of the esplanade at the northern end of Surfers Paradise was swept away. In the quiet weather that followed, the sand was driven shorewards and the beach gradually regained its normal profile and a wave-break bar but it took three years. The damage triggered a major rethink on how to manage our beaches and eventually resulted in the construction of the A line and artificial reefs.

Some years ago a team of scientists, including two from local Griffith University, studied the impact of major storms on Broadbeach, south of Main Beach, but not dissimilar to it. During the period of study Broadbeach experienced three storm erosion events. Offshore buoy measurements were used to estimate wave conditions. The first storm over three days in early March 2006 was a hybrid-cyclone which generated one of the most energetic wave conditions on the Gold Coast of the previous 30 years, with measured offshore significant wave height reaching 5.3 metres, and maximum wave height 10.7 metres at the Gold Coast Seaway buoy opposite Main Beach's Spit. During two other later storm events, wave conditions were much less energetic than during the first storm, with significant wave heights ranging from two to three metres. The severe early March storm resulted in an average of 48 cubic metres eroded from each metre of the beach and a 70 metre seaward migration of the outer bar in just a few days.

Main Beach experienced another succession of intense storms between 2009 and 2013. To remedy severe erosion, the City Council delivered just over three million cubic metres of sand to Palm Beach and from Miami to Main Beach as part of the Beach Nourishment Project from June to September in 2017.

It also decided to look into some way of protecting Narrowneck specifically, as it is amongst the most vulnerable stretches of beach to erosion on the Gold Coast It was decided that an artificial reef would likely be an effective solution. Several options were looked into. The final design chosen was in the shape of a split V, with the northern arm longer. The reef was originally built of some 400 specialised large fabric sand bags, each 20 metres by 4.5 metres. The filled bags were deposited in an elaborate GPS controlled operation to make sure the reef was as close as possible to the design. The resulting reef is 450 meters long by 250 meters wide at the top of the V. The work was completed by December 2000. This proved to be very effective at heading off and slowing the movement of sand northwards along the beach and also slowing the amount of wave energy that has the potential to remove sand during storms.

Narrowneck reef

Subsequent monitoring shows that it has continued to be a success. So in 2018, a renewal project was kicked off to extend its life. An extra 84 of the mega sandbags were placed around the original reef. Two yellow navigation buoys next to the reef were also installed to prevent damage from anchoring vessels. A study found that, depending on the tide, waves between 0.7 – 2.0m high were breaking on the reef and that there were waves breaking on the reef roughly half of the time.

Local surfers say there is no doubting the artificial reef improved the quality of waves in the immediate vicinity, and as a result Narrowneck is now one of the more popular surfing beaches on the open stretch of beach, though some say the impact is diminishing. Further analysis has shown the beach in the shadow of the reef was approximately 20 metre wider than areas unaffected by the presence of the reef. An added bonus is that, like all artificial reefs, it is now home to all sorts of marine life, including corals, fish and turtles.

Narrowneck wave

Main Beach cannot, of course be separate from regional influences. It exists within a wider environment that few parts of the world's coastlines can match. We have a rare combination of features present in south eastern Queensland and northern New South Wales: plentiful sand, a warm sea current and mild winters. And several rocky headlands that shelter some beaches in southerly weather.

- o O o -

The sea

The beach of course would be much less memorable without the sea; it would be more like the Sahara Desert. And oh those waves, spawned well out to sea, rolling in relentlessly; sometimes furiously, sometimes very gently. Sometimes breaking up in messy whiteness, sometimes as stunning barrels, an offshore wind pulling at their peaks, causing a gentle spray.

It as if the sea has moods. Sometimes its feisty, other times it is calm. Sometimes it looks as though it is trying to make up its mind how it feels, before settling into a groove. This is of course all anthropomorphic nonsense. But the sea is a part of we humans' DNA. For thousands of years we have lived by the sea, fished in it, sailed on it for trade, exploration and war. From the Minoans of Crete of 4,000 years ago and the Polynesians of the Pacific Ocean around the same time, to the great sea battles of the Second World War, the sea has been integral to our lives. It has inspired great works of literature, art and music. Moby Dick, Lord Jim, The Cruel Sea: Fantasia on British Sea Songs, including Britain Rules the Waves sung so energetically at The Last Night of the Proms, to the Beach Boys' Surfing USA, and any number of paintings of ships at sea or in harbour. Today we may have moved on a little but we are still captivated by ocean events, like the Sydney to Hobart yacht race or the America's Cup, or the giant waves of Nazare in Portugal and Hawaii's Banzai Pipeline.

But it also has a darker place in our psyche. Symbolically, the sea has long been seen as hostile and dangerous where scary creatures lurk in the depths. There is the gigantic Leviathan sea serpent reported in the Bible, the huge shark-like sea monster Isonade of Japanese mythology and the ship-swallowing Kraken that supposedly patrolled the waters off Norway terrorising the vikings. And the ancient Greeks revered the capricious gods and their acolytes like the god of the sea Poseidon and his sea nymph wife Amphitrite. These days we have moved on, though today's holiday makers my have replaced the old myths with an unreasoned fear of sharks (more of that later).

* * *

Main Beach is on the Coral Sea, which takes its name from the coral formations of the Great Barrier Reef, the largest known reef system in the world, and over a thousand kilometres north of the Gold Coast. The Coral Sea extends southwards to about Coffs Harbour at 30 degrees south of the Equator, where it meets the Tasman Sea. Just over 300 kilometres north of Coffs, at 28 degrees south, Main Beach comfortably fronts the southern section of the 2000 kilometre long Coral Sea.

The Coral Sea is dominated by the Eastern Australian Current, which originates from the South Equatorial Current. That is driven across the Pacific Ocean around the Equator by the easterly trade winds until it bumps into Northern Australia, where it is deflected south along the east coast of the continent. The Eastern Australian Current is a warm stream that also receives a large dose of warm water from the Great Barrier Reef lagoon. It flows as a continuous stream along the edge of the continental shelf to Sea Rocks, just south of Forster in New South Wales, where it breaks up into a series of anti-clockwise rotating whirlpools up to 100 kilometres in diameter.

The warm Eastern Australia Current brings warm nutrient-poor waters down the coast to the cool waters of the Tasman Sea.

It is the strongest of all the currents running along Australian coasts and transports 30 million cubic metres of water per second at about seven kilometres an hour within a band about 100 kilometres wide and 500 metres deep. It is strongest around February, when the water temperature reaches 24° Celsius and weakest around August, when water temperature drops to 19°C. It gets cooler as it travels south. It is rather warm and stable at 27–28°C in the north all through the year. The salinity of the water is about 35 grams of dissolved salts per kilolitre, which is about the global average for sea water. The water is mostly very clear, with visibility of about 30 metres near the reefs.

Having said all of that, the warm Eastern Australia Current does little to influence Main Beach ocean wave patterns, but does have an impact on the general climate. We can thank it for our balmy summers and mild winters.

Although wave patterns can in theory be created by any kind of disturbance in the water, there are three primary natural causes: wind, earthquakes, and the gravitational pulls of the Moon and Sun.

Wind waves are the most familiar kind; they are also the most variable and, in many ways, the most puzzling. The size and variety of the waves raised depend on three main factors: the speed of the wind, the distance it blows across the water and the length of time it blows. The faster the wind is blowing and the stronger it is, the greater the size of waves. The longer the wind blows at the same speed and direction the larger the waves will become until what is called a fully risen sea is reached. And then there is the fetch; the longer the stretch of water the wind can blow the larger the waves. But the character of the waves changes markedly as they move away from the winds that created them.

These factors tend to be a stronger influence on the shore north of Fraser Island (K'gari), than they do further south. A larger contributor to the wave energy of Main Beach and the Gold Coast in general is the ocean swell generated in the southern Coral and Tasman Seas and Southern Ocean. These tides, which are a special kind of very long wave, are caused by the Earth's rotation under the great bulges of water raised by gravitational fields of the Moon and Sun.

Without doubt, the most important phenomenon for producing waves Gold Coast surfers ride is the low pressure, also called the mid-latitude depression or extra-tropical cyclone. The low pressure is really just a cell of air whose pressure is lower than its surroundings. However, thanks to the Coriolis force (the Earth's rotation), it also features a swirling pattern of fast-moving surface air, which generates waves on the sea by transferring energy from the air to the water, The greater the pressure difference between the centre of the depression and the surrounding air, the faster the air moves. The faster the air moves, the more energy it imparts on the water and the bigger the waves will be. In deep water, waves do not carry water from one place to another, They are not like ocean currents. Waves are simply carriers of energy. Imagine rippling a carpet: energy moves from the hands shaking it to the other end, but the carpet surface itself does not move.

The Coral Sea tidal wave arrives first at Point Danger on the border with New South Wales from the southeast and reaches Main Beach about half an hour later. Generally, high and low tides occur about one hour later each day.

Regardless of the mechanism by which a wave is generated, the character of the waves and the velocity at which they move are influenced by the depth of water in which they are travelling. Waves 'break' as they enter shallow water. The friction of contact with the sand slows the bottom of the wave while the top pushes on, eventually 'breaking'. Conditions on the day, as well as the slope of the beach, affect their breaking profile - or the shape when looking side on. Experts have calculated an average ratio of sea depth to wave height that leads to a 'break', with the stress on average. The ratio is about 1.3 times the height of the wave. That means that a typical one metre wave will break in about 1.3 metres of water. Surfers will tell you however, that the rule is almost totally academic, as there are so many exceptions that they don't 'prove the rule'. But it does help tell us about how a wave breaks. If a wave breaks in water of less than 1.3 times its height, then its profile will be steeper and more hollow. But if the wave breaks in water whose depth is more than 1.3 times its height, it will be flatter and more gently sloping.

One thing that the breaking depth - and so also the wave profile - depends upon is the suddenness with which the the depth changes as the wave heads towards the shore. If the transition from deep to shallow water is gradual, the wave tends to break round the 1.3 times rule. This delivers a slow, gentle breaking wave. In contrast, if the transition from steep to shallow water is sudden, for example over an offshore reef   (like the one at Narrowneck), then the wave finds itself momentarily over very shallow water without having broken. This makes the wave suddenly increase in size at the same time as the water depth suddenly decreases, so the height of the wave is relatively large for the depth of the water. It is also makes the wave steep, hollow and fast, and much loved by experienced surfers.

The afternoon offshore breeze physically holds up a wave, stopping it breaking until it gets into shallower water. That is why there are more tubes when the wind is offshore. An offshore wind also 'cleans up' the swell itself, removing the short-period wind-generated sea and leaving the long-period swell waves. A strong onshore wind also has a double effect. It causes the waves to spill over early, making them break into deeper water. With onshore wind, the waves are guaranteed to break more slowly and with less power.

* * *

Main Beach has a gently sloping beach but significantly it has two sand bars running parallel to the shore line: one close inland is usually attached to the beach, the other is further out - around 200 metres to 250 metres from the waters edge. These have a significant impact on our waves. If you sit and watch for a while you often see waves breaking around about where the outer sand bar is, and then something gentler and more modest happening right close to the waters edge. The outer sand bar waves are usually types known as the 'plunging breaker', which are more powerful and generally the best for surfing, with a possible tube. It is also why the artificial reef off Narrowneck is usually a good spot for surfing.

Those outer bar waves can be rough, and not for the inexperienced surfers or swimmers. The energy of waves increase with their height, but it is not a linear progression. For example a two metre high wave has four times as much energy as a one metre wave, and a three metre wave is ten times more powerful than a one metre wave.

Breaking waves travel at between 10 and 15 kilometres per hour - Olympic swimmers can swim at around seven kilometres per hour. White water, known as wave bores, travels at between three and seven kilometres per hour.

There is a wave buoy opposite Philip Park, just north of the Sheraton Grand Mirage on the Spit, floating atop 17 metres of water that has measured the top ten wave heights since it was installed in February 1987 (and upgraded four years later to use a computer-based system.) As a wave monitoring buoy floats up and down each passing wave, its motion (or heave) is measured and electronically processed. The data is downloaded every hour, which accounts for the time stamps in the table below.

Now, clearly a 12 metre wave is pretty huge; not unlike a four story building hurtling towards you. But it's not the biggest. The highest wave ever recorded in Queensland waters was off North

The flat beaches of Main Beach

Stradbroke Island in the same 24-hour period in March 2006 as Main Beach's third largest ever. It was measured at a whopping 16.8 metres high. The North Stradbroke buoy that survived such violent sea sits atop 80 metres of water. It was generated by an intense low pressure weather system centred 135 kilometres east-northeast of Cape Moreton. And when Main Beach reported it's biggest ever way - 12 metres - there was one at Tweed Heads to the south that came in at 13.1 metres.

The Highest Waves recorded at Main Beach (off the Spit)

Rank	Date and time	Height metres
1	3 May 1996 6.30 am	12.0
2	17 March 1993 4.30 am	11.0
3	5 March 2006 5.00 am	10.7
4	22 May 2009 12.30 pm	10.6
5	5 March 2004 10.00 pm	10.6
6	12 June 2012 7.00 am	10.5
7	28 January 2013 9.30 am	10.5
8	25 April 1989 9.30 am	10.0
9	15 February 1995 10.30 am	9.2
10	4 June 2016 10.00pm	9.1

And then there are rips, which every lifeguard will tell you to avoid. Where there are waves there must also be rips. Rips are nothing more than a way the water gets back into the sea after it has arrived at the water's edge in waves. Along Main Beach there are rips about every 200 metres or so.

They are dangerous for the uninitiated. I'm told there is a tendency among some of the uninitiated, mostly tourists unfamiliar with our beaches, to seek to enter the water where the waves appear less daunting. They may be reluctant to enter where there are lines of whitewater rolling towards the beach (a natural mechanism for returning poor swimmers to the land), but be keen

to enter the water where the waves aren't breaking so violently, oblivious to the seaward-flowing torrent ready to carry them well beyond the reach of those waves. Rip currents under average wave conditions, where the waves are under 1.5 metres high, travel at as much as five and a half kilometres per hour. An average rip in a surf zone 50 metres wide can carry you outside the breakers in as little as 30 seconds.

That is why it is essential for people to swim in water on beaches that are watched over by a lifeguard, who has assessed that section of beach and placed red and yellow striped flags maybe 20 metres or so apart that designate the safest spots, though of course the water off these beaches can be fierce everywhere.

Because the water depth is never exactly the same along a stretch of shore, waves are drawn to areas of shallower water and away from areas of deeper water, even if the difference is very small. Once beached, so to speak, the water will naturally gravitate to the spots of lower pressure and from there flow back out to sea. These rips can stay in place for several weeks at a time but their configuration can be wiped out by a fierce storm or large swell.

But there is one part of Main Beach where there is always a rip, and it is a particularly dangerous one. That is south of the seawall at the northern end of the Spit, where there is a very strong undercurrent and rip moving from north to south as the waves crash into the seawall, the water must head south to get back out to sea again. Sometimes the sand floor is unpredictable too. Recently, for instance, it was reported that there was a full drop off, where the water goes from being 30 centimetres deep to 2.5 to three metres deep within just a metre or so of sand underfoot. The undercurrent then connects to a strong rip that runs out away from the shore, right through the pylons of the sand bypass jetty and it has a zone which often stretches for about 20 metres on either side of the jetty itself. As that rip sucks through the jetty area it can swirl and bend, creating undertows and reverse currents as well. But, and this is a big one, the area often looks gentle and calm on the surface, enticing in the unaware.

Before we leave this section, there is one other phenomenon worth noting. You occasionally see foam on the beach. It is common around the world and usually not dangerous, although in some cases it can include toxins from, for example, human pollutants. When foam gets particularly thick it can cause visibility problems for surfers and swimmers. The foam is formed by the agitation of water by wind and waves. Seawater contains many particles of organic material, such as fats and proteins from the algae and animals that live in the ocean. Algal blooms, waves crashing through kelp forests or surf stirring up sediments all lead to higher than usual amounts of these organic materials in coastal waters, and can result in the formation of sea foam. We see it only occasionally on Main Beach.

Very occasionally you see brick red colour water close in to shore. It is seen after especially turbulent times and is the result of the churning up of the seabed immediately beyond the water line. Most days you go down to the water's edge and paddle in the glorious clear water of Main Beach's stretch of the Pacific Ocean.

- o O o -

Beachcombing

Shells

Main Beach's beaches are awash with shells. All shapes, sizes and colours. The ones we see easily are nestled in patches along the sand just beyond the water's edge, as if in a beauty parade with the more handsome ones expecting to be picked up by a delighted child.

In reality, of course, they are, or more correctly have been, the hardened external skins of a wide range of molluscs, which are soft body animals such as sea snails, clams, cockles and scallops, mussels and rock oysters that grow the shell as a safe haven for themselves. Seashells are created through the secretion of proteins and minerals of these creatures. The secretions form layers that harden into shells. The colourings result from the creatures' diets. This process of how shells are made is what creates such personality in each one. They are different from snail to snail even within the same species.

There are altogether about 100,000 species of molluscs, of which about half live in salt water. And they are found all over the world. All molluscs have a brain, digestive and a reproductive system. Nearly all lay eggs and some even look after their eggs after laying. After hatching, many of these tiny marine animals are lava-like and have a free swimming stage before changing into miniatures of their final form, growing their shells. Technically a tough shell is called an exoskeleton, which has helped protect the mollusc from predators and the unforgiving sea. When these animals die, or moult (which is the process of shedding the shell in order to grow bigger), the shell is left behind and sometimes washes up on the beach.

Mollusc poking out of its shell

If you look closely enough at a group of Main Beach shells you will see that there are two main types. There are the flattish ones, and the spiral or conical ones. The flattish ones are known as bivalves. Bivalves have two similar parts or valves, that swing open from their base where they are joined with a ligament hinge. Usually we only see one half washed up on the beach as the waves have split them, but sometimes we can see the two halves still linked together. On their own, they often look like the logo of the famous oil company, Shell, which when you think about, is an odd name for a company that drills for oil and gas. It is also the shape and design often seen in art: think Botticelli and *The Birth of*

Venus painting, where the goddess arrives naked out of the sea riding on one half of a very large bivalve shell.

Some bivalves, such as mussels and rock oysters, are attached to hard surfaces and can't move around. You see them on the rocks at the Seaway on the Spit, for instance, or around the base of Broadwater marina piles. Most bivalves are filter feeders, sieving organic particles from the water.

Bivalves are usually regular in outline either with the right valve convex and the left side slightly concave, or more or less equivalved. They are generally sculptured with radiating ribs which sometimes carry small spines. The beak generally has an 'ear' on each side, the front one, the larger. They swim, apparently haphazardly, by rapid opening and shutting the valves, especially to escape their main predators, starfish.

Equally important is the action of waves. The churning effect of waves on the shore tends to keep sediment (silt, sand, gravel, shells and rocks) suspended in the water, preventing it from settling. The stronger the waves are, the bigger a chunk of sediment must be to avoid getting moved around by the waves. This means that the waves sort the sediment: fine silt tends to collect where the waves are weak, and gravel and rocks will be deposited where the waves are large. Seashells are relatively large and heavy, but they're also flat and not at all aerodynamic, so the surf sorts them with relatively coarse sand and fine gravel. You rarely find shells sorted with fine sand or silt, and only very large shells end up with cobblestones. That is why on Main Beach, as elsewhere, you see batches of shells nestled in slighter coarser sand, and then stretches of finer sand without shells.

I haven't see this myself but I'm told that sometimes you will see bivalve shells that have a small hole drilled into them, as though someone has already prepared them for stringing on a necklace. Yet the holes are not the result of something we have done, in all likelihood they have been made by an octopus, partial to a mollusc. If the octopus can't prise the two valves of the shell apart, it will bore a small hole through the shell, pushing through with its salivary papilla (a fleshy mouthpart, the tip of which is lined with small teeth), releasing a toxic venom that helps dissolve the calcium carbonate of the shell and poisons the animal inside. It's an operation that requires patience: boring through a shell might take an hour or two.

The second group of shells, the conical and spiral ones, house gastropods, commonly known as snails. There is a huge diversity of gastropod species - over 62,000 have been named - but even within a single species there can be a large range of shell colours and patterns. Some marine snails are squat and rounded like garden snails, and others are tall, thin, conical like ice-cream cones. They may have spiralled shells, or simple tent like shells, such as the limpet, whose shell resembles a low-rise teepee or a hat with straight ridges radiating from a central point.

These snails are called univalves, as they have just one main shell part. They come in a range of shapes from classic spiral snail forms to flatter, open-based abalone (a mollusc with a shallow ear shaped shell lined with mother-of-pearl and pierced with a line of respiratory holes) and limpets (a shallow conical shell and a broad muscular foot clinging to rocks). Some species have an operculum, like a plate which they use as a hard door to close the shell opening. Opercula are flat on one side with a spiral pattern; those on turban snails are colourful and sometime called "cats' eyes".

Gastropods generally grow by adding to the edge of the tube which is coiled, usually dextrally (i.e. with whorls rising to the right and coiling in an anti-clockwise direction).

Generally those living in warm waters are more colourful than those living in cold. They have a ribbon-like set of teeth, the radula, which they use like a file to eat their food. Some are vegetarians, some carnivorous and some are scavengers. Many marine snails are good at surviving exposure to air and warmth, and are common in the intertidal zone, which can get hot when exposed at low tide.

* * *

Whatever the practicalities of nature, seashells have long held deep symbolic meaning for people of many cultures. In the islands of the south Pacific, they were often used as currency and tools. In art and literature they are often associated with love and fertility. Medieval Christian traditions associate seashells with pilgrims. In some new age traditions, seashells are used to symbolise the unconscious and are associated with emotions. Their connection to the sea and water evokes peace and tranquility. Among other attributes in Feng Shui tradition, keeping a basket of shells in your home will bring good luck. I like to think that the shells on Main Beach have brought me tranquility.

Shells are important too for First Nations people living near the shore. Shells of mussels were often traded and used as tools, either to make fishhooks or to scrape animal hides and wood. In some areas, shells were used in ceremonies, such as initiation and other rituals and as body ornaments. Women in particular collected shells and used some of them to make necklaces. We do not have evidence of what happened at Main Beach, but we do know there was extensive trade in shells in pre-European settlement Australia. A necklace uncovered with cremated remains in Tasmania was found to be 1,800 years old. It consists of 32 rainbow kelp shells each pierced with a small hole.

Shell collecting remains as desirable today as it has been for thousands of years. People still stroll along the beach fondling prized selections in their fingers before either returning them to the sea or slipping them into a pocket for safekeeping. The calming effect of rummaging through washed up shells will last as long as there are shells to collect.

* * *

You'll see a range of objects other than shells on the beach. There's a term - beach wrack - for this. It refers to the items that you may find washed up on the beach. Commonly found wrack on Main Beach includes cuttle bone, squid shell, goose barnacles and razor shells. You may also find Blue Bottle Jellyfish (more of this later), 'By The Wind Sailor Jellyfish', and Porpita, usually at the same time because the wind and ocean currents bring them onshore collectively.

Almost anything that has spent at least several weeks drifting near the surface of the ocean will have goose barnacles attached. Barnacles are often mistaken for molluscs (the group that includes snails and mussels) because of their hard external shells, but they are actually crustaceans (related to crabs, lobsters and krill) that as adults are sedentary - in other words they stick in one place. They have cirri, appendages like legs that resemble a fan or rake, which they sweep through the water to collect particles of food.

Goose barnacles are 'stalked' barnacles - their shells make a flat, teardrop shaped compartment at the end of a fleshy stalk. Some goose barnacles grow on rocks on the edge of the shore. An interesting feature that barnacles have evolved to deal with restrictions of being attached to a surface, unable to move around to find mates, is to have a disproportionately long penis. Some barnacle penises can extend to more than eight times the animal's body length - handy for reaching out to the sexy barnacle over on the next rock.

Jellyfish and other Nasties

Australia as a whole is home to a variety of potent jellyfish, however due to the cooler waters around Gold Coast, compared to further north, jellyfish on Main Beach are quite rare. In fact, the numbers of jellyfish found regularly in the region are so few that most people would say that the Gold Coast does not have a jellyfish season, but rather a few days each year when jellyfish stingers are sighted in the water. Sometimes we do need to be on the watch for nasty stingers, however. Floating hydroids with stinging tentacles, known locally as Bluebottles or Portuguese Men of War (on beaches off the Atlantic coast), occasionally drift at the surface of the ocean and are often blown on shore, sometimes in mass strandings. Strong on-shore northeasterly winds and warmer currents bring the armadas (which is what a group of bluebottles are called) to the east coast of Australia on the incoming tides. There was a remarkable and very unusual swarm of bluebottles in January 2019 when 476 stings were recorded on a single Sunday afternoon of terror. A Surf Life Saving officer on duty that day described the scene as an "epidemic", the like of which he had never seen before. Unusually strong north-easterly swell conditions pushed the bluebottles onshore and they were clumped in their thousands along the shoreline, so much so that lifesavers were forced to close a number of beaches.

washed up bluebottle

The sting of the bluebottle can be painful and can cause an allergy-like reaction in some people. If there are many fresh bluebottles on the beach it is probably best not to go swimming, since more are likely to be washing in. You should also watch where you step, as the tentacles can still sting while wet on the beach. Dried out bluebottles are generally okay to touch and you can handle a living bluebottle safely by holding its sail, the gas-filled bladder. It is probably of some comfort to know that there has been no recorded fatality from a bluebottle sting in all of the Southern Hemisphere.

Each bluebottle is not a single organism. It is actually a colony made up of several individuals that have specialised roles in reproduction, feeding and defence. Some form tentacles that dangle down in the water and catch passing fish with venomous staging cells or nematocysts, which immobilise the prey. The tentacles then retract, pulling the prey up to the feeding polyps (other individuals in the colony), which digest them. At the top of the colony, above the cluster of reproductive and feeding polyps, is the sail. In bluebottles the sale is shaped a little like the bag of a set of bagpipes and tapers to a point at either end. In some colonies the sail may be so large that it extends up to 15 cm above the surface of the water.

The sails have a slight twist to them. Some twist to the left and others to the right. Several hypotheses have been put forward to explain why there is this left/right difference in sails. There is no doubt however, that the twist affects where the animals go. They depend entirely on the wind to move, but some move to the left of the downstream wind direction while others move to the right, meaning that colonies head off in different directions when the wind blows. This dispersal probably helps them to maximise access to food resources so they're not all feeding in the same place, and would also help safeguard against having them all wash up and die on the same beach at the same time.

There are also the very occasional appearance of other jellyfish. These sea creatures generally cannot control their movement, except how high they are in the water. Otherwise they are at the mercy of currents and tides. In January 2015, a very large swarm of blue jelly fish appeared about 400 metres offshore in a 50 metre wide band that extended from the Seawall to Narrowneck. No-one, though, came to any harm.

There are more venomous jellyfish in Australian waters. There is for example the Box jellyfish or the very small Irukandji jelly fish, both of whose venom may well prove fatal for humans, but they do not stray south of tropical waters and are not a threat at Main Beach.

- o O o -

The big three of our seas

The majestic plains of Africa's Serengeti National Park are said to house the big five of the wild. These are generally agreed to include the lion, the elephant, the leopard, buffalo and rhinoceros. Australia has nothing comparable in the wild, but we do have majestic sea animals. Main Beach regularly sees what we might call the Big Three.

Dolphins

Like seashells and other sea creatures, real and imaginary - think mermaids - dolphins have a rich association with many cultures. Because they often guided lost or stranded fishermen home, sailors saw in the dolphin the human qualities of love, affection and friendship, and as providing warnings of imminent danger. In Christian symbolism dolphins have been seen as an aspect of Christ and a symbol of resurrection.

Even before the Christian era, you can see pictures of dolphins on the walls of old Roman cities, like that of 3,500 year old Knossos on the island of Crete, where there are wonderful friezes of blue dolphins, carefully restored a hundred years ago. Dolphins were much revered by the ancient Greeks and Romans, for similar reasons as the early Christians.

They have been equally part of local culture. It is said that the Quandmooka First Nations people of Stradbroke Island (Minjerribah) had dolphins help in the hunting and fishing. On sighting a shoal of mullet, the fishermen would beat the water with their spears to alert their dolphin helpmates, to whom they gave individual names, and the dolphins would then chase the shoal towards the shore, trapping them in the shallows and allowing the men to net and spear the fish. Some traditions have it that this practice was shared by the Kombumerri clan of the Yugambeh language group, who lived on the Gold Coast around Main Beach. The dolphin is known to have played an important role in a legend of the Nerang River, according to which the cultural hero Gowonda, who after his death, was reincarnated into one.

Dolphins regularly visit the Gold Coast and Main Beach, and there is a resident population of them here. Higher densities of dolphins have been found near estuaries. There are resident pods around Currumbin Creek and the Tweed River to the south. On Main Beach they live around the Seaway, and further north at Jumpinpin - the waterway between North and South Stradbroke Islands. They forage in the Broadwater and canals, eating a wide variety of fish, mostly, with the occasional mollusc as a tasty alternative, perhaps as an appetiser. It has been estimated that there are about 550 dolphins living in Moreton Bay, about 172 in southern Moreton Bay.

Various species of dolphins have been spotted throughout the year but the most abundant are Indo-Pacific bottlenose. These grow to 2.6 metres long and weigh up to 230 kilograms. They are born about one metre in length and weigh between nine and 21 kilograms. Their backs are dark grey and their bellies are lighter grey or almost white with grey spots. They got the name Indo-Pacific because they inhabit the coasts of India, eastern Africa as well as northern Australia. They can hang out in groups of hundreds, but mostly they are in groups of five to 15. A charity group called Dolphin Research Australia that has been conducting regular observations for a decade or so, reckons there were around 17 individuals about ten years ago, mostly females. Griffith

University researchers have estimated that they have been in the region for at least 30 years. Many of the adults identified a decade ago are still in the region, according to more recent observations.

Calves can be born throughout the year after 12 months gestation, but Dolphin Research Australia says there is a peak in births during the warmer months of late summer through to autumn. A bottlenose dolphin calf remains dependent on its mother for two to four years, and reaches sexual maturity after eight to ten years if female and ten to 12 if male. They can live for over 50 years. The Broadwater pod of female dolphins is very tightly bonded. They regularly forage and feed throughout the Broadwater. They have been seen foraging as far as 15 kilometres up the Nerang or Coomera Rivers chasing prey, but they always come home.

Dolphins suffer from shark attacks, entanglement in shark nets and fishing gear, and boat strikes. These events leave marks on their large curved dorsal fins, making it possible to identify individuals. Dolphin Research Australia shows a dozen dolphins on their web page. There's a male named Snoopy, there's another male called Hutch, and, obviously, another male called Starsky. There are females Muppet, Lynni, Patti and Smudge. Poor old CJ, a youngster, has the most damaged fin, missing its tip and sliced almost through on what's left. They can be very active at the surface and can be seen leaping, surfing and tale slapping.

Mature males often form a strong bond with at least three or four other males. The females live in larger groups and interact with network of other pods within their home range. This bonding is no doubt helped and strengthened by their ability to communicate with each other. Bottlenose dolphins make a wide range of sounds, including echolocation or sonic clicks, and burst pulse sounds such as 'squawks' and 'squeaks'. Whistles seem to be used to keep in contact with each other, to identify and locate others. Bottlenoses apparently have 'signature whistles' which are unique to individuals and are pretty much like a name.

courtesy: DolphinResearchAustralia

* * *

Australian humpback dolphins, a little larger than their bottlenose cousins, are also regularly seen off the Gold Coast. They can be distinguished from their cousins by their long slender beak and low triangular fin. The live in smaller groups, maybe four to five individuals. The males hangout together, as do the females in somewhat larger groups. They are tropical creatures and the Gold

Coast is about as far south as they come. Investigations by Dolphin Research Australia have revealed that some individual humpback dolphins have lived in the area for at least 10 years. Just how many humpback dolphins there are on the old Coast is currently unknown, but was thought to be around 128 individuals in 2016.

Then there are short-beaked common dolphins in these waters, but usually further out to sea in open waters off the continental shelf, occasionally wandering closer to the shore. They are smaller than the bottlenose. Their dorsal fin has a pointed tip and concave trailing edge. They are grey, black to brownish on their upper side. They are also probably the most playful of the species, very acrobatic. They are often seen porpoising, leaping, tail slapping and headlining. They often approach vessels to bowride, which is similar to a surfer catching a wave. They are often seen in photographs swimming alongside ocean liners.

Nowadays the love for dolphins lingers, and we are all uplifted when we see them up close. They bring joy to the heart.

Sharks

Renowned Hollywood film director Steven Spielberg recently said he regretted the impact of his 1975 movie "Jaws". He told a British Broadcasting Corporation Desert Island Discs radio programme that he fears sharks are "mad" at him for the "feeding frenzy of crazy sword fishermen that happened after 1975". The film has been blamed for misrepresenting Great White sharks and leading to trophy hunting, especially in the United States. The key problem "Jaws" created was to portray sharks as vengeful creatures. The story revolves around one shark that seems to hold a grudge against particular people and goes after them to kill them.

The author of the book on which the film was based, Peter Benchley, was deeply perturbed by this. He said years later that "knowing what I know now, I could never write that book today. Sharks don't target human beings and they certainly don't hold grudges". He spent much of the rest of his life, he died in 2006, campaigning for the protection of sharks.

There are estimated to be about 50 species of sharks that inhabit the waters off Australia's East Coast. Marine biologists say it is impossible to calculate an accurate number of species and sharks in the region; it is more a case of educated guesswork. They do say that over the past fifty years the numbers of large sharks are in decline. Off Main Beach and the Gold Coast, scuba divers commonly see harmless leopard sharks and wobbegong (also known as carpet) sharks, shark rays, guitar sharks but encounters with large sharks around Gold Coast waters are very rare, even though most divers would love to see one and so are actively looking out for one. From scuttlebutt and social media it seems there have been only a handful of sightings between Moreton Bay and Byron Bay over the past decade. Though it is said that better technology in the form of patrolling drones and the ubiquitous mobile phone camera is now increasing the number of sightings, but there hasn't been an increase in the number of incidents.

The headline grabbing sharks - the Great Whites of "Jaws" fame - are very rare. Using some innovative methods, the Commonwealth Scientific and Industrial Research Organisation (CSIRO) has found that Australia has two white shark populations, an eastern population ranging east of Wilson's Promontory in Victoria, to central Queensland and across to New Zealand, and a southern-western population ranging west of Wilson's Promontory to Western Australia. Their research indicates that there are about 750 adults in the eastern Australasian white shark population (though it could be as few as 470 or as many as 1030), and about double that number in the southern-western population. It takes 12 to 15 years for these legends of the sea to reach maturity. CSIRO estimates that the total number of white sharks in the eastern population is 5,460, though there could be as few as 2,900 and as many as 12,800.

The Great White shark is one of the world's top of the pile predators, much like the lions on the plains of Africa. They are also one of the world's largest predators, they can range in length from three to six metres, with white bellies and dark grey fins and the classic pointed snout. Great Whites roam the continental shelf waters, and have been responsible for shark bites. While Great Whites are large and potentially lethal predators, they are not necessarily more dangerous to people than other shark species. They tend to be very elusive and shy, and divers say it is extremely difficult to encounter one naturally, even as a professional, and even more unlikely that they will voluntarily approach humans in any setting. Encounters with Great Whites most often result from being in an area with a high volume of their food or other bait. There are videos online of Great Whites attacking cages suspended from boats off South Africa, but the waters have been specifically baited to attract them.

* * *

The Tiger Shark is a scavenger that will eat a wide range of prey and even indigestible objects. Turtles, sea snakes, crustaceans, cephalopods, small sharks and fishes are common meals and perhaps surprisingly also oceanic pufferfishes. They have also been known to ingest seabirds, marine mammals, jellyfish and marine iguanas. Due to its large size, scavenging nature and shallow-water feeding, Tiger Sharks are considered dangerous to people, but actual attacks have been few and far between. They can be recognised by their blunt head, serrated cocks-comb-shaped teeth and their colouration. Small juveniles are grey with dark reticulations, which change to vertical bars in fish up to three metres in length. The bars may be faint or lacking in individuals longer than three metres.

Bull sharks, on the other hand, are more aggressive and considered to be one of the most dangerous species. They are found all over the world. In Gold Coast waters, bull sharks are the most dangerous and aggressive shark found quite commonly in these waters, and often seen in the canals. They often feed in murky water so that they may be around in shallow water at the seaway after a storm has churned up the rivers and streams. They eat almost anything: other sharks, dolphins, rays, fish, turtles, birds and molluscs. They can and do penetrate freshwater river systems and have been known to take cattle, dogs and people.

They are stocky sharks, weighing between 90 and 200 kilograms and grow to between two and three metres as adults. They have strong jaws, a very large bite pressure and can be easily provoked. Plus, their habitat overlaps with that of humans more than other large sharks, which can lead to higher numbers of encounters and bites. Some experts even say it takes the top spot on the list of dangerous sharks over both the Tiger and the Great White, due to its particularly aggressive behaviour.

Two other species are sharks are regularly seen around Main Beach and the Gold Coast.

The Leopard shark is easily recognisable and frequently encountered by scuba divers. It is so named because its colouring resembles that of a leopard, with light coloured body and dark spots. Leopard sharks grow to two metres, and are slow swimmers. Unlike the African beasts they are named after, they are not aggressive or dangerous to humans.

Leopard sharks are nocturnal and spend most of the day resting motionless on the sea floor. At night, they actively hunt for molluscs, crustaceans, small bony fishes, and possibly sea snakes inside holes and crevices in and around a reef. Though solitary for

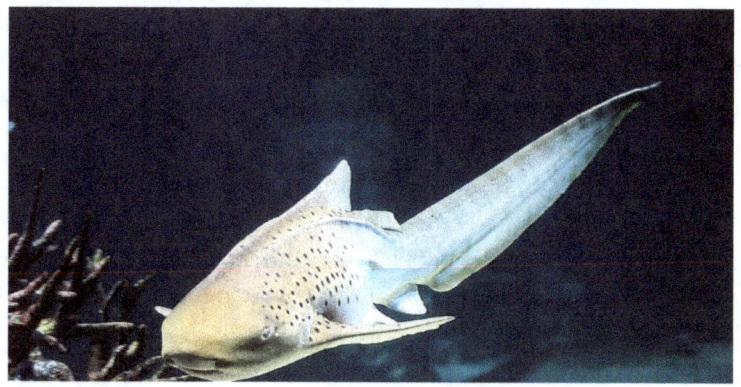

A leopard shark

most of the year, they do form large groups in some seasons.

Another common shark is the Wobbegone, also known as the carpet shark, because it's a bottom feeder. The name wobbegong is believed to come from a First Nations language, meaning "shaggy beard", thanks to the growths around the mouth of the shark of the western Pacific. They are thought to be only found in Australian waters. They are a relatively large shark that hang out near the bottom of shallow water, and can reach up to three metres in length, though more usually they are about 1.25 metres long. They have a flat, blotchy-coloured body and skin flaps around their snout. Their colouring ranges from sandy and brownish to a bright rust. Similar to leopard sharks, wobbegongs are a regular sight for divers. There are a few different species of wobbegong, including the spotted wobbegong, banded wobbegong, and banded carpet sharks. None are considered dangerous to humans. There have been a few instances of divers getting too close and being bitten, but there have not been any fatalities.

Whaler sharks are some of the more normal-looking sharks - or at least the ones that conform to our expectation of what a shark looks like - found in the area. They also have one of the wider distributions: these lengthy grey sharks with narrow, streamlined bodies are found extensively throughout Australia's coastal waters, including along the Gold Coast. Whaler sharks spend most of their time in deeper water along continental shelves, and are found at depths up to 400 meters. These pointy-snouted sharks are predators for fish and even other sharks, and while they do inherently pose a danger to people, very few dangerous whaler shark encounters have been recorded.

One of Australia's best known and indeed iconic shark species is the Grey Nurse shark. It is now listed as endangered. Recent research estimates there are about 2,000 grey nurse sharks living along Australia's east coast, however, the breeding population consists of just 400, the mature males and females . There are known groups north of Main Beach off Double Island Point and off Moreton and North Stradbroke Islands, but none known to be here on a regular basis. In any event, they are slow swimmers and not notably aggressive.

* * *

But sharks are predators. Marine biologists argue that their behaviour needs to be understood and respected. Unlike crocodiles, sharks are not opportunistic hunters and will not hunt people down in the water. They are not vindictive like the fictional Great White in "Jaws". A shark when fed, will preserve its energy for times when it needs to hunt again or defend itself. In a nutshell, encountering a shark is very rare and encountering one that is actually hunting at the same time is even more unlikely. Most incidents between sharks and humans are related to mistaken identities where surfers or swimmers are bitten on the surface. These incidents often end with a single bite as the shark usually notices that it is attacking something outside its usual diet. Attacks on scuba divers are almost unheard of unless the circumstances involve bait in the water, spearfishing, shark feeding activities or provoking the shark. Many, many surfers paddle across the Seaway on their boards from the Spit to South Stradbroke Island every day, right over the top of a known bull shark hot spot on the northern rock wall and yet there are no known incidents involving humans and sharks there.

Overall, shark attacks at the Gold Coast are extremely rare — records indicate only one unprovoked attack every couple of years, and only three fatal attacks since the year 2000. Gold Coast's lakes and canals seem to be more dangerous than the main beaches, but even so, shark attacks there are uncommon. A man died after a bull shark attack in Miami Lake in late 2002, and there was another fatal attack in early 2003 in Burleigh Lake. The lakes are close and are part of the same canal system. A surfer was attacked and died off Greenmount Beach in Coolangatta in 2020. There have been no known attacks off the beaches of Main Beach. The closest was a fatal attack at Surfers Paradise in 1958.

Some marine biologists argue that sharks know what they are doing, and when they come into contact with humans, it might be that they see the human as competition for food and might try to frighten him off with a bite. There are no known cases of sharks actually eating a human.

Whales

Then there are the lumbering giants of the sea. The largest animals on Earth. We have them in abundance off Main Beach as they migrate north and return south every year.

We have become accustomed to hearing how many species in this world are in danger of extinction. Take the koala, for instance; a species in serious jeopardy because of urban encroachment and bush fires. Whales, on the other hand, have experienced a wonderful recovery from being a direly threatened species. It is a great success story.

For hundreds of years around the world whales were hunted commercially. In Australia, commercial whaling started in 1791, with the closest whaling station to Main Beach at Tangalooma on Moreton Island, about 85 kilometres north as the crow flies. This single whaling station hunted down, killed and processed 6,277 humpback whales between 1952 and 1962. That's almost two of these gentle giants every single day of the year. In fact, this was what is somewhat euphemistically called overfishing, and, with other stations, contributed to the collapse of the humpback population, to the point where they were close to extinction in the southern oceans by the early 1960s. The Tangalooma station closed in 1962, and, in 1965 Australia banned whaling altogether, 174 years after it started.

From a low of about 500 humpbacks travelling up the east coast past Main Beach in the mid 1960s, we now have more than 20,000 of these 40-tonne mammals making the journey from their Antarctica feeding grounds each year to breed, calve, and frolic in the warmer waters of the Coral Sea. Some estimates are as high as 40,000 each year. It is reckoned that at least one third visit the Gold Coast bay and pass by Main Beach during their migration.

After the massive decline in the numbers of all types of whales and with fewer mouths to feed, the Antarctic krill stocks increased and there was plentiful food for the few animals that survived. The steady growth of about ten percent of the krill stocks each year over the past decades has started to level off in recent years, and is expected to soon see a slowdown in the steady increase in the whale population. Perhaps, and we certainly hope, it will settle at a naturally sustainable level.

The whales we see off the coast at Main Beach are humpbacks, who belong to the family of baleen whales known as rorquals. Baleen is a filter-feeding system inside the mouths of baleen whales. To use baleen, the whale opens its mouth underwater to take in water, then pushes the water out, and animals such as krill are filtered by the baleen and remain as food for the whale.

An adult humpback is between eleven and 17 metres long, weighing between 25 and 40 tonnes. The newborn calves are four to five metres long and weigh one to two tonnes. Females tend to be a metre or so larger than the male. It's difficult to tell a male from a female as they both have internal sex organs. Humpback pectoral fins can be up to a third of the body length (around three to five metres) and have a series of humps called tubercles on the leading edge. The dorsal fin is located about two thirds of the way back from the tip of the rostrum (what marine biologists call the flat upper jaw) and is low and broad based, often sitting on a raised hump of tissue more obvious when they arch their backs to dive.

The tail flukes have a serrated trailing edge, which, along with markings on the underside of the tail fluke, can be used to identify individuals. The rostrum is also covered in golf ball sized tubercles. Each tubercle has a stiff sensory hair or vibrissa around 1.2 to 2.6 centimetres long which has a rich blood supply and is connected to a nerve suggesting a function as a sensory organ – perhaps to detect current and temperature changes in the water to aid in navigation.

Humpbacks are black or dark grey on the upper dorsal side and they generally have large amounts of white on the underside of their body, pectoral fins and tail flukes. Southern Hemisphere humpbacks tend to have more white on the underside of their body which extends further up the sides of their body. The unique black and white markings on the underside of the tail flukes are like fingerprints in people with no two being the same.

The appearance of our humpbacks is distinctive. They have long pleats (or grooves - known as ventrals that enable the lower jaw to expand) that run from the tip of their snout to their navel on the underside of their body and a flat upper jaw. Long pectoral fins distinguish humpbacks from other baleen whales.

Humpbacks, too, are the most acrobatic of the larger whales, amongst the most exuberant of all whale species and, fortified by the food-rich waters of the Antarctic, they arrive ready to breed, which they do are around the Whitsundays area, feed and frolic. August and September are traditionally their more playful months. They regularly breach, lob their tails, slap their pectoral fins and raise their bodies half out of the water to see what is going on (known as spy hopping). They often do high energy full body breaches where their whole body is out of the water. They are most active in their breeding grounds around the Whitsunday's region, but are frequently seen cavorting off Main Beach. Adults usually dive for between ten to fifteen minutes to a depth of about 120 metres, followed by three to four blows - up to four metres high - at the surface at 15 to 30 second intervals as they fill their lungs with air, much like a snorkeller. Before a deep dive, they usually raise their wing-shaped tails (called flukes) at the surface, known as a 'fluke up' dive. They have a cruising speed of eight kilometres per hour, but can reach a speedy 32 kilometres per hour for short bursts.

These majestic animals like to swim in shallower parts of the ocean, with a depth of less than 200 metres. They come particularly close in at the Gold Coast, generally within 20 kilometres of the coastline but often much closer, because there are some of the narrowest sections of the east coast continental shelf at the Gold Coast bay.

Griffith University's Coastal and Marine Research Centre scientists say that as an open bay, the Gold Coast is a particularly appealing destination along the east coast migration route. It is a spot that humpbacks can easily access if they want to leave the Humpback Highway for a break or to socialise. There are similar bays along the migration route used by humpbacks but they are either not with in easy reach for us to watch them or are less accessible for the whales themselves, so there are not the same high numbers of animals in those bays.

There is also some evidence that the Gold Coast is a favourite area for mothers and their new born calves. One group of researchers observed 2,305 humpbacks between 2011 and 2017 collecting information from trained observers on whale-watching vessels. They recorded 74 newborns, with most seen in July and August. These findings may indicate that the Gold Coast Bay provides a particularly attractive habitat for calving for the humpbacks.

The researchers analysed seasonal presence of mother-calf pairs, dive times, direction of movement and location to work out the use of the bay as a resting area. On average a quarter of all sighted whales were mother-calf pairs with peak sightings each October. The recorded average dive time of 3 minutes 20 seconds was short compared to that in the migratory corridors. Mother-calf pairs were sighted more often closer to shore relative to other pods. The researchers compared their results with recognised breeding and resting grounds and they were found to be similar. All-in-all, the researchers concluded that the Gold Coast bay may serve as an important stop-over for humpback whale mother-calf pairs.

* * *

Occasionally completely black individuals are seen in eastern Australian waters, and an all-white individual has been a regular visitor here in the past. He, we do know it's a he, has been named Migaloo, which means "white fella" in some Aboriginal dialects. He is an adult reckoned to be born in 1986, so he is now in his late 30s, the prime of life for a whale. He is one of just a handful of known white humpbacks worldwide — and the most famous. There are three other known white humpbacks. Willow lives up in the Arctic and was spotted along the coast of Norway in 2012. Bahloo lurks in Migaloo's territory in the Great Barrier reef, and was first seen in 2008. But these two are not as gregarious as Migaloo, rarely showing their faces. In 2011, a nearly all white humpback whale calf was sighted in the Whitsundays. This whale became known inevitably as Migaloo Junior, even though it is not known to be the offspring of Migaloo – they may or may not be related and only genetic tests could confirm this. He was first spotted as a youngster in 1991 passing through Byron Bay, and again two years later in Hervey Bay. With brown eyes and his white skin, he isn't hard to spot in a pod of humpbacks. His pigmentation is likely a genetic mutation, and scientists have speculated whether he is a true albino or if he is leucistic: which is a condition that makes for an inability to produce pigment but with coloured eyes. At the time of writing, he hasn't been seen for a few years, the last time was 2018, also off Byron Bay heading towards Queensland. Marine biologists have said that Migaloo may have started to swim further offshore as he has matured, making it possible that we'll see less of him over the coming years.

They know he's a male from his song. While both male and female humpbacks make sound, only males sing the melodic humpback songs. In 1998, researchers first recorded Migaloo singing and you can hear it online (at https://soundcloud.com/iwhales/migaloo). That he is a male was confirmed in 2004 by DNA tests after researchers from Southern Cross University collected shed skin samples left floating on the sea surface after Migaloo had breached and continued his journey south.

Migaloo's tail

That humpbacks sing has been known for some time but some newish research by the University of Queensland shows they learn quite tricky tunes from other regions. Study leader Dr Jenny Allen says whale songs change every year, and the researchers have found neighbouring whale groups are learning each other's distinct tunes. The whales in eastern Australia sing a particular song pattern, and then the next year, whatever was sung in eastern Australia, the New Caledonia whales will be singing too. So, the song is learned from one population to another. The study examined songs of male humpback whales from eastern Australia and New Caledonia between 2009 and 2015 to decipher how culture transmits between the populations.

Dr Allen said it showed the whales learnt quickly and with remarkable accuracy. "What we found was that they don't have to make it dumbed down at all," she said. "They can keep it as complicated as it was originally, and they're able to learn the whole thing. Both populations have a shared migration route that goes past New Zealand on their way to Antarctica." Dr Allen said there were some places where the singing was easy to hear, but unfortunately for Main Beach residents, the best spots are at their breeding grounds around the Whitsundays area. That's where they sing the most. It would be nice to think the males are serenading the females; perhaps they are.

All humpback whales are protected under Australian law, but Migaloo and other humpbacks that are more than 90 per cent white are "special management marine mammals" and have extra protection: boats and vessels cannot approach within 500 metres and aircraft cannot approach within 610 metres. Migaloo was struck by a boat in 2003 which left scars on his back.

* * *

Whales and climate change

Nowhere on Earth seems likely to escape at least some impact from climate change during this century. The Bureau of Meteorology says Australia's climate warmed by almost 1.5 degrees celsius between 1910 and 2020.

The Gold Coast is vulnerable to sea level rise, but it won't be Main Beach carrying the brunt of the problems created. Experts have identified Paradise Point and Runaway Bay, both north of Main Beach and somewhat ironically more exposed to the Broadwater as most at risk.

But Main Beach will not likely get away scot free.

Griffith University's Coastal and Marine Research Centre, reckons the increasing number and intensity of severe weather events caused by climate change pose a challenge. The Centre says that the wet and windy La Niña years will increase relative to the dryer El Niño. During a La Niña, cyclones tend to form closer to the coast. Warmer water might cause tropical cyclones to form further south or track further south. This could result in changes to the 'wave climate', which pushes sand north along the coast and helps to naturally replenish eroded beaches. These future trends are notoriously hard to predict. We could see more longshore drift or less. Yet so far, at least, Main Beach and the Gold Coast has adapted to changing conditions. But future variations of wave direction and frequency and intensity of events may have quite severe short term effects.

But while there is no doubt in my mind that we as a society need to take action to combat and adapt to climate change, there is some good news.

Recent research has shown that whales act as highly effective carbon neutralisers. A study has made the case that not only did the whaling industry of the 19th century rob the world of some of nature's most awesome creatures, it also robbed us of a useful tool against climate change.

Although whale populations are now recovering, they are estimated to be only a fifth of those before industrial whaling, according to the paper in the journal *Current Biology*. This is a pity, the authors of the research say. Through living, excreting and dying — naturally rather than on the end of a harpoon — whales are able to lock up large amounts of carbon, they argue. Consequently, they say, climate change is yet another reason to work to increase their numbers.

Blue whales are the largest animals that have existed, reaching 200 tonnes — equivalent to more than 30 elephants — in weight. About a fifth of that, or 40 tonnes, is carbon. The humpbacks that we see off our coast are smaller but still big enough to make an impact. This means that just by existing, a blue whale has removed the equivalent of two and a half times the average Australian's annual carbon footprint. It also means that if the global population of whales returned to its pre-industrial equivalent we would remove, the researchers estimate, 17 million tonnes of carbon. Then, every time one of those whales dies, it falls to the bottom of the ocean, where that carbon can be locked up for good.

However, researchers believe this is a small part of the contribution that whales make to carbon sequestration. To support their great bulk, whales have to eat a lot. This means they have to excrete a lot. Because they also travel a lot, they spread this around the ocean. When they do, they also spread nutrients. Previous research has shown that this supports populations of smaller creatures such as plankton, which provide 'considerable pulses of carbon' to the seafloor. Quite how much, they still don't know..

The International Monetary Fund (IMF) of all people have gone into bat for whales and the benefits they bring to our climate. A recent paper trumpeted that "when it comes to saving the planet, one whale is worth thousands of trees.

"The carbon capture potential of whales is truly startling. Whales accumulate carbon in their bodies during their long lives. When they die, they sink to the bottom of the ocean; each great whale sequesters 33 tons of carbon dioxide on average, taking that carbon out of the atmosphere for centuries. A tree, meanwhile, absorbs only up to 48 pounds of carbon dioxide a year.

The IMF says that wherever whales are found, so are populations of some of the smallest phytoplankton. These microscopic creatures not only contribute at least 50 percent of all oxygen to our atmosphere, they do so by capturing about 37 billion metric tons of carbon dioxide, an estimated 40 percent of all carbon dioxide produced. "To put things in perspective", the IMF says, "we calculate that this is equivalent to the amount of carbon dioxide captured by 1.70 trillion trees - four Amazon forests' worth".

The IMF concludes with what might be called a wish. "If whales were allowed to return to their pre-whaling number of four to five million - from slightly more than 1.3 million today - it could add significantly to the amount of phytoplankton in the oceans and to the carbon they capture each year. At a minimum, even a one percent increase in phytoplankton productivity thanks to whale activity would capture hundreds of millions of tons of additional carbon dioxide a year, equivalent to the sudden appearance of two billion mature trees. Imagine the impact over the average lifespan of a whale, more than 60 years."

The bushlife

The original inhabitants around and near Main Beach were the Kombumerri clan of the Yugambeh language group. It has been said that their clan name translates as the mudgrove-worm people. And I have seen a suggestion that they called the Main Beach area Kulgeragah (or Kijeragah), after the kaloon tree. And there is archeological evidence that they had lived hereabouts for tens of thousands of years. It was estimated that between 1,500 and 2,000 people lived between the Logan and Tweed rivers, including the Nerang River mouth. Unfortunately very little of their pre-European settlement activity has been recorded, so we do not have a comprehensive picture of what the natural environment looked like, but we do know that they lived off the land and water. Like their neighbours on North Stradbroke Island, of whose history more is definitively known, they lived on an abundance of shell fish, particularly a seawater clam called yugari and other fish, dugongs and turtles. Their subsistence patterns followed seasonal variations. From April to July, fish were (still are) abundant - especially whiting, bream, tar whine and catfish. Mullet, salmon and tailor were especially plentiful in the cooler months around June and July through to September, spawning in the estuaries. There were also many land-growing delicacies to be enjoyed including honey from wild bee hives, and soft grubs.

Yet the lush vegetation of these bygone times is now scarce, at least in its original form. If you see old aerial photos of Main Beach in mid-20th century you will initially be struck by the absence of high rise buildings that now dominate the suburb, with several more going up as I write. But as you look to the edges of the frame you will see sand, and lots of it. MacIntosh Island Park is a sand island. The Spit is a narrow peninsula between the ocean and the Broadwater. It too is just sand, having, as we saw earlier, been host to the constantly north-moving mouth of the Nerang River.

The once sleepy Gold Coast became Australia's tourist mecca in the 1950s. Prior to that, during the early years when Southport was the urban centre of holiday fun on the Gold Coast, visitors were ferried across the Broadwater to surf at Main Beach. The area became more popular after the construction of the Jubilee Bridge in 1926 which ran roughly east-west over the Nerang River to directly to Main Beach when land was taken up and people started building holiday houses and beach shacks. Some guest houses also sprang up but few people lived here permanently. Evidence of the area's popularity as a surfing beach remains in the form of the Main Beach Pavilion built in 1934. From mid century development began to take off. The construction of the new north-south bridge and the deviation of the Gold Coast highway to the west of Main Beach in the late 1960s was preceded in the 1950s by early reclamation of the Nerang River to the west of the earlier subdivision, and the area centred on Tedder Avenue dates only from that time. The next three decades saw phenomenal development. Hotels, canal estates and apartment blocks were built at a roaring pace, carving through the natural bush. Sand mining at Currumbin, Broadbeach and Main Beach's Spit had already compromised the natural environment of the region. In the 1940s, and especially during World War Two, silica and mineral sands were mined at the Spit for industrial production. There were large deposits of rutile, zircon, ilmenite and monazite. Areas were revegetated after mining.

Only the Burleigh headland well to the south of Main Beach remained as natural, original bush on the region's coastal strip. Everything else, especially the greenery around Main Beach has since been reintroduced by people. MacIntosh Island is a green oasis, mostly inhabited by native trees and plants, with its man-made lake and stream flowing through the centre.

What you now see on the Spit is also man-made, or at least man-started. It too has been stabilised and transformed into a green corridor along the shoreline. About forty years ago, after decisions were taken about the construction of the Seaway and as a result locking into one place the mouth of the Nerang River, the City Council set up a beach protection program and planted trees and shrubs, and an automated irrigation system, along the Spit in order to quickly stabilise its coastal dunes rather than rely on the often haphazard and slower ways of unguided nature. Over 15,000 specimens have been planted including tuckers, banksias, blueberry ash, coastal pig face and soap trees.

Now, we have the Federation Walk through the revegetated strip which fully opened in 2003, that enables us to enjoy this reinvented literal forest. The authorities, not unreasonably, now claim that the natural areas "are managed as environmental reserves in which natural values prevail. Coastal vegetation communities that historically occurred on the Gold Coast are fully established, [and] support biodiversity".

The Spit's natural areas are now home to native species endemic to the coastal landscape of the Gold Coast. Sand dunes are the dominant landform along the Gold Coast coastline. These long stretches of sand are interspersed with rocky headlands. Prior to European settlement, more than 850 hectares (approximately one per cent) of the Gold Coast's land was what is called 'exposed coastal'. These days it is estimated that more than 90 per cent of exposed coastal areas have remained intact or have been restored.

The revegetated areas of the Spit are now a good example of coastal rainforests that once existed close to the beaches, such as the Surfers Paradise rainforest that once grew between Main Beach and Broadbeach. The coastal rainforest that grows on the basalt rock at Burleigh Heads is another type of littoral rainforest and is the only example of this type on the Gold Coast. It has a relatively low species diversity compared to other types of rainforest. Only a few patches of the original remain. Now the relatively new littoral rainforest has been created on The Spit to mimic how much of the coast used to be.

Strolling along the shaded Federation Walk you will encounter birds and lizards, drawn back by the richer pickings now on offer. But, rest assured, none of the most commonly seen animals and reptiles are dangerous to humans.

The most common birds you will come across will be the Australian bush turkey rummaging around in the twigs and undergrowth. They may be cautious at first but are not especially intimidated by people so you can get reasonably close to them, though I can't see a reason to do this. Mind you, it is prohibited to feed the bush turkeys and in any event our snacks will not do them any good.

You may also see brown quail scuttling around in the underbrush. Among the trees, the soft coo-oo calls of various types of doves let you know they are around, and you will probably hear the laughing kookaburra long before you see it. There will probably be the brilliantly coloured rainbow lorikeets out and about. This bird is unmistakable with its bright red beak and colourful plumage. Both sexes look alike, with a blue head and belly, green wings, tail and back, and an orange/yellow breast. They are often seen in noisy and fast-moving flocks, or in communal roosts at dusk.

You might see a galah or two. They are easily identified by their rose-pink heads, neck and underparts, with paler pink crown, and grey back, wings and under-tail. They spend much of the day sheltering from heat in the foliage of trees and shrubs.

Then there are rosellas. They are medium-sized colourful parrots with distinctive white cheek patches. They have a red head, neck and breast, with yellowish to greenish upper parts, a yellow underbody and a yellow-green to blue-green rump, with a red under-tail. The shoulders are bright blue. They use one foot (usually the right one) to hold food when eating on the ground or perched on a tree. Other common birds include fairy-wrens, white-naped honeyeaters, sea eagles and whistling kites. Carpet snakes have also been found, though I have never spotted one here.

There is a Friends of Federation Walk webpage that you can google, which does not seem to have been updated for several years. It lists up to six dozen birds that can be seen along the walk at various times. My experience is that there is no chance of seeing more than a few of them during any one walk and you will hear more than you actually see.

You may see bearded dragon lizards basking in the sunshine on the walkways, blending in perfectly with the fallen leaves. They tend to be perfectly still, until you get close when they scurry away. Bearded dragons have broad, triangular heads, flattened bodies, and rows and clusters of spiny scales covering their entire bodies. Their name comes from the underside of the throat of the lizard, which can turn black and expand for a number of reasons, most often as a result of stress or if they feel threatened. Apparently some people keep them as pets.

Main Beach is not especially renowned for its instincts for conservation. After all, outside our capital cities' central business districts there may be more high rises per hectare than anywhere else in the country. Thankfully, though, there is now a master plan in place for the Spit, protected by Queensland legislation, that will surely protect the rejuvenated natural areas for the foreseeable future.

* * *

In the Broadwater, to the east of the Spit, off Doug Jennings Park at the northern end, you can see Curlew Island. It is about a kilometre south of Wavebreak Island and it falls within the Spit Master Plan area. This unprepossessing sand island is said to be one of the most significant environmental sites in the whole of the Gold Coast Broadwater. It is a safe haven for scores of birds, including long range migrators. Sometimes up to 1,000 shorebirds and seabirds gather there. It is the roost and feeding area for large numbers of migratory birds that travel half way around the world, and for Australian shorebirds, terns, gulls and other species. These birds require a high tide roost site and Curlew Island is regarded as a critical roost site for these birds. A number of major studies and data confirm its importance.

The island is classified as "significant" under environmental protection laws for the number of migratory birds, including Eastern Curlews, Bar-tailed Godwits, Double-banded Plovers and Whimbrels that make their way there every year. The Broadwater has a large population of migratory waders. These birds make long annual migrations between Australia and the northern hemisphere.

The migratory waders seen on the Broadwater, span the globe with their migration journeys. They leave in March and April and fly to northern polar lands where they breed. They return to the Broadwater in September and October. During the Australian summer they recover and rebuild themselves for next year's journey. Their round trip is between 16,000 and 20,000 kilometres. Sometimes they have known to fly for several days at a time without landing along the route.

In January 2018, a combined wader count recorded 995 shorebirds from 11 species including those migrating birds already mentioned. Bird counts taken at Curlew Island over three years up to 2018 show that it has a permanent population of between 40 and 80 Eastern Curlew (which are critically endangered) and a similar number of Bar-tailed Godwits. At the same time, on the western side of Wavebreak Island, which because of vegetation cannot be seen from the Spit, about 500 shorebirds were observed.

The eastern curlew is Australia's largest migratory bird. It spends its summers in Russia and its winters in Australia. It is a large wader with a very long down-curved bill that is dark brown with a pinkish base. This bird is dark-streaked and has a long, heavily streaked dark-brown neck and whitish chin and throat. Its legs and feet are long and blue-grey. It is a bulky bird, weighing almost a kilogram. This bird feeds in the tidal zone and then moves to sand dunes and open areas at higher tides to roost, which is why Curlew Island is so appealing, not least because it is cut off from land-based predators.

Back in 2007 a Bar-tailed Godwit hit the headlines, after a bird known as E7, was recorded flying non-stop from Alaska to New Zealand — a journey of more than 11,500 kilometres - in just 11 days. It was a world record, with the information collected by a tiny satellite transmitter attached to the bird's back. Although E7's globetrotting feat was widely acclaimed around the world, and stood unsurpassed for years, the record has been broken a number of times since then by another Bar-tailed Godwit with a transmitter.

And in 2022, the record has fallen yet again, to another Godwit, a juvenile this time, which flew an even more astonishing distance of 13,560 kilometres from Alaska to Ansons Bay, on the north-eastern coast of Tasmania. That distance is longer than E7's epic journey by around 2,000 kilometres (to put it into perspective, the extra stretch it covered is about the same as the distance between

Speedy Bar-tailed Godwits

Melbourne and Noosa). And this non-stop flight was also completed in just eleven days. Indeed, this bird had ample opportunities to stop over for a feed and a rest on a number of tropical islands as it winged its way south across the Pacific Ocean, but chose to keep on flying. It has been said that the total cumulative distance flown over a lifetime by a Bar-tailed Godwit on its annual migration between Australasia and the northern hemisphere would equate to flying to the Moon and back.

* * *

We live on the southern edge of Main Beach on the Macintosh Island reach of the Nerang River. We look out over the river and onto Macintosh Park. Along the river mangroves have grown back. Although the park is not officially in Main Beach - the City Council has it formally in Surfers Paradise North, though one of its web sites notes that Macintosh Island Park is a real oasis in the midst of all the glitz and glamour of *Main Beach* (my italics, obviously) - we think of it as ours. We walk there very often. Part of it, around an artificial lake among the mature trees, is a bird sanctuary, home to flamboyant peacocks and peahens that roam through the parklands. There is also a gaggle of impressive looking white geese.

On most afternoons, if you keep a keen eye out, you will see several largish birds - about 60 centimetres from tail to beak - grey-brown in colour standing, sometimes sitting, remarkably still. They are well camouflaged, which is why you need to keep your eyes peeled. They are Bush Stone-Curlews. These large, charismatic birds spend almost their entire lives on the ground, although adults can apparently fly well. They hunt by night for small animals, lying or sitting still by day among leaf litter, where their plumage provides superb camouflage. According to the Birds of Australia guide book, the loud, eerie wailing of the Bush Stone-Curlew is one of the characteristic sounds of the bush, especially in northern Australia. They nest on the ground, making their chicks vulnerable to being taken by foxes and dogs. But the parents' size and impressive threat display are possibly enough to ward off all but the most determined predator.

Our favourites, or the ones that have claimed our hearts, are the family of Black Swans. We first saw the two parents and three small chicks in mid-August last year. They swam past us: Mum or Dad in front, then the three chicks, and Mum or Dad bring up the rear. The youngsters are not black, they are a sort of fluffy dirty grey.

The guide book says that Black Swans are natives of Australia, sort of diametrically opposite of the White Swans of the northern hemisphere. They are entirely black except for their white flight feathers, red bill and red eyes. Pairs are common even on

Bush Stone Curlew

ornamental ponds and urban lakes, and huge flocks may gather at
moulting sites where the birds become flightless for about a month
after breeding. The Black Swan is a powerful flyer and its
distinctive nasal bugling can sometimes be heard as the birds fly
overhead at night.

Our swan family seems to be based on the edge of a small sandy
beach on the north east of Macintosh Island. Everyday they
venture westward along the river en famille, often coming ashore
on the parkland along the southern side of Hill Parade, there to
fossick around for a while before heading home. Black Swans are
mainly vegetarian, upending in the river to graze from submerged
vegetation.

"Our" black swan family

While it is heart warming to watch the growing family and the devotion of the parents, who, if someone gets too close, get a bit uppity, flapping their wings, stretching their neck forward and creating a noisy ruckus, there is a dark side to nature. Another pair of black swans had built a nest nearby, a large mound of reeds, grasses and weeds a bit over a metre wide and half a metre high, hoping to raise their own family. The male of our family took exception to this development, presumably seeing it as an encroachment on his territory, and constantly attacked and disrupted the preparations of the second pair, who ended up trying to hatch eggs that had died through lack of uninterrupted care. Eventually, Council Park staff removed and disposed of the dead eggs to free up the second pair to resume normal life. We suspect they have gone somewhere else to try and raise a family, as we have not seen them for months. Apparently Black Swans often migrate to new areas and create nests at any time in the year when conditions are favourable.

After hatching, the cygnets are tended by the parents for about nine months until fledgling, during which time they grow to be as large and as black as their parents. Our family is now pretty much all grown up, just six months after we first spotted the young cygnets. The kids are as big as Mum and Dad though still have a touch of grey on their backs.

A flock of sea gulls is also a part of our local community. These silver gulls are the most common members of the Australian gull family. They are a small, graceful bird with a silvery back, pure white underparts and a red bill, legs, feet and eye-ring. They hang out usually in a group on the beach at the end of Breaker Street, sometimes as many as a hundred, occasionally a few of them sit on the water, just beyond where the waves are breaking. On the beach they sit and stand, occasionally molested by an excited child. One or two fly off, perhaps in search of food, while another few fly in to join the group. These gulls feed out at sea and apparently often require a rest during the day, though this is probably fanciful. They probably rest when they have had enough to eat. There is a small group of them, perhaps two dozen, who seem to have made the sandy beach on the river in Macintosh Park as their base of operations.

The species has become a common urban bird, scavenging for scraps at picnic tables, beaches and parks, and appears to be increasing in population around large cities. Silver gulls lay one to three eggs in a nest of seaweed and other vegetation, which may be constructed on the ground, in low vegetation or among boulders or even marine debris.

We were concerned for our MacIntosh Island flocks during the noise and crowds generated by the re-established Gold Coast Supercar racing around the streets. There was much disruption for all of us, especially the birds. However, all seemed to return to normal once the petrolheads had departed.

- o O o -

The weather

'Beautiful one day, perfect the next' was a slogan used in a tourism advertising campaign by the Queensland government. Climate change and the La Nina/El Nino weather phenomena might disrupt that from time to time, but it remains broadly true, thank goodness. As mentioned earlier, we can largely thank the warm Eastern Australian Current that flows past Main Beach for that. But that is not whole story.

To understand Main Beach weather and climate we need to go back to basics for a moment. The sun's rays kick start our weather, providing both light and heat to Earth, and regions that receive greater exposure warm up more. This is what happens in the tropics, which see less seasonal variation in sunlight. Moisture-laden tropical air warms, becomes less dense, and rises. But as air reaches the upper levels of the atmosphere, it cools. Water molecules condense to form clouds and eventually fall as rain. Warm air rising from Earth's surface pushes the air mass away from the equator, and releases its moisture as rain as it travels towards the poles. As warm air rises in the tropics, cool air is drawn from surrounding areas to fill the void. This creates the trade winds that blow in subtropical regions. Air circulates from the tropics to regions approximately 30° north and south latitude, just south of Main Beach (we are at latitude 28°), where the air masses sink. It is why northern New South Wales gets so much rain.

These basics explain why weather forecasts are dominated by the atmospheric pressure zones that push and pull air and moisture around. For Main Beach, in summer the high pressure zones are concentrated around 36 degrees south around Kangaroo Island in South Australia, which allows an equatorial low to centre itself over west-central Queensland. The counterclockwise flow of air around the zonal highs pushes a southeasterly flow of humid Coral Sea air onto the east coast, which is boosted by the pull of the inland low pressure. The moist air brings humid conditions and summer rain to the east coast and Main Beach.

In winter the high moves north to 30 degrees south, still centred well below the Queensland border. For this reason, Queensland is largely impacted by the northern, and in particular the northeastern section of the high pressure systems, which delivers a broad strong flow of southeast to easterly air, originating in the Coral and Tasman Seas. The southeast trades are the most dominant features of Queensland weather systems, and the source of most of the wind and wave energy along the east and gulf coasts, including Main Beach, particularly in the winter months. While the highs produce the most dominant winds on the coast, their low to moderate velocity results in the generation of only 10 per cent of waves in excess of 2.5 metres

In fact, records show that storm waves in southeast Queensland are driven by topical cyclones 27 per cent of the time; by east coast cyclones 47 per cent of the time; by mid-latitude cyclones 14 per cent of the time; and by anticyclonic highs trade winds 10 per cent of the time.

We do have beautiful sun-filled skies much of the time but with so much water around it is inevitable that we also see a lot of cloud activity. Many people are not aware that the water vapour that makes up clouds is not like the mist from a sprayer nozzle or steam from a kettle. Each droplet of water in a cloud is much, much smaller. It is only a millionth of a millimetre in diameter. Millions would fit into the full stop at the end of this sentence. When billions and billions of them congregate, they build the huge, fantastic shapes we call clouds. That's why a typical cloud - a puffy, small fair weather cumulus measuring a few hundred cubic metres, contains only a bathtub's worth of water.

Yet cloud droplets aren't the smallest form of aerosolised water. They coalesce from even smaller, airborne molecules of evaporated water much less than a millionth of a millimetre in diameter. The warmer the air, the more evaporated water it can hold; the cooler the air, the less evaporated water it can hold. There comes a limit, the dew point, when relative humidity levels reach 100%, or complete saturation. Only then can cloud droplets form (they also need microscopic particles of dust to seed them - without dust, there would be no clouds). The dew point can be hundreds to thousands of metres above the ground. Or it can be just a few centimetres. Fog is a cloud creeping on its belly.

All of this technical detail can obscure the fact that Main Beach enjoys year round good weather. The coldest month is July when the maximum temperature is 20 degrees celsius and the nights a sleep-inducing 9 degrees minimum. January is the warmest month when the average temperature hovers between a high of 28.8 degrees and a low of 21.9 degrees. On average there are 9 days in January when the temperature reaches above 30 degrees. Humidity is what can make hot days really uncomfortable, and the relative humidity hovers around an average 70 per cent most of a January day. Sea breezes tend to blow away the worst of that by afternoon on Main Beach. In fact, these breezes are more frequent and intense in the summer months.

It is the warm weather and the high pressure zones that generate these sea and land breezes. The sea breeze results from the warming each day of the land around the coast. The air above the land warms up and begins to rise. As the land gets hotter and more air rises, air moves in from the relatively cooler coastal ocean waters. As a result, a local circulation cell is set off, with the cooler sea breezes replacing the hotter land air. At night and in the early morning, the opposite often happens, as the now cooler land air replaces the higher warming air over the ocean. This produces a light offshore breeze, more common on clear, still mornings. The direction of the sea breeze at Main Beach is mostly southeasterly.

Despite the sophisticated computer models of various weather forecasters, east coast cyclones are not all that well understood, yet they are the ones that wreak most havoc on Main Beach and south east Queensland generally. They can develop at any time of the year but are most prevalent in early to mid winter. They usually last for four or five days and are highly variable in frequency, with some years having only one east coast cyclone and others may have several. They generally form off the Central Coast region of

New South Wales just north of Sydney and quickly intensify, possibly reaching the strength of a tropical cyclone. They then meander southwest over the Tasman Sea. When near the coast they produce very strong winds, heavy rainfall and big seas and swells. They are responsible for about half of high waves (over 2.5 metres) along the southeast coast.

In summer, mid-latitude cyclones tend to be kept south by the High Pressure System and have very little impact on Main Beach weather. Their arrival is usually heralded by a cold front, accompanied by strong west by south winds and at times some rain. As the lows pass, the following highs take over, as the winds tighten and tend more easterly. These lows are, however, responsible for the low to moderate southeast swell that arrives along the southeast coast.

Of course averages can be misleading, because by definition there is generally something higher and something lower than an 'average'. Also, at any one time, we may be in an El Nino or La Nina year. These eastern Pacific weather patterns off South America have a big impact on our weather. In fact the tropical Pacific Ocean and atmosphere swing between warm, cool and neutral phases on a timescale of a few years. El Nino events, which usually lasts for one year, produce dryer, warmer weather; La Nina, which can last over several years, brings heavier than usual rain, generally cooler temperatures and more cyclones. There are also so-called neutral years when neither of these systems are present. Since 1900, there have been 27 El Niño and 18 La Niña events in Australia.

So while we should beware of averages, they do provide flavour of usual weather patterns So here's a summary of our average weather through the year:

Summer

The average maximum temperature in December, the first month of summer, is 28 degrees celsius, though obviously some days are hotter than this. The average maximum temperature peaks in January at 29 degrees, and eases off in February back to 28 degrees again. The relative humidity for the year peaks in February, averaging 77 per cent. The minimum average temperatures hover around 20 and 21 degrees.

The highest temperature recorded at Main Beach was 40.5 degrees on 24th February 2004. February usually sees seven days when the temperature is above 30 degrees.

Rain days, where more than one millimetre falls, increase in summer to between nine and 11 days rain as we get to February. February has the highest average annual rainfall at 190 millimetres.

Summer is the windiest season. It's not straight forward to characterise 'average wind'. The Bureau of Meteorology uses the 'daily wind run', which is an indication of the average wind speed over a 24 hour period. This shows that the average daily wind run is just over 20 kilometres per hour in December, rising to just over 22 kilometres per hour in February. The maximum wind gusts will be higher than this. The maximum wind gust speed in summer recorded in the past 20 years was 98 kilometres per hour on 28th January 2013.

A typical, or average, January day when half of the country is on holiday will see a temperature of 26 degrees at 9 am, with a relative humidity of 70 per cent. The wind would be 18.6 kilometres per hour from the south or southeast. At 3 pm, the temperature would be 26.6 degrees, the relative humidity unchanged while the wind would have picked up speed to 25.5 kilometres per hour, still from the south-east.

Autumn

March doesn't feel much different from summer temperature wise, with the maximum at 28 degrees and the minimum at 19. It starts to cool down in April and May with the tops 26 degrees and 24 degrees respectively and minimums slipping to 17 and 14 degrees.

After an average of 12 days rain (again of more than one millimetre) in March, we slip to an average of nine days rain by the last month of autumn. The wind speed drops from about 21 kilometres per hour and the beginning of the season to around 17 kilometres per hour as it draws to a close.

Winter

The word winter conjures up cold and damp in many parts of the world but not on Main Beach. June and July see average temperature highs of 21 degrees and just five or six days when more than one millimetre of rain falls. The monthly minimum temperatures start at 11 degrees in June, then slip to 9 in July, the coldest month of the year, and begin to ease back up in August to 10 degrees. August sees the lowest relative humidity of the year at 67 per cent. The coldest day recorded on Main Beach in the past 30 years was 2.5 degrees overnight on 19th July 2007.

July records the lowest annual average rainfall at 51 millimetres. The wind eases from summer, hovering around 17 kilometres per hour most of the time.

A typical, or average July day will see a temperature of 16.5 degrees at 9 am, with a relative humidity of 61 per cent. The wind would be 13.7 kilometres per hour from the north-east or the south. At 3 pm, the temperature would be 19.7 degrees, the relative humidity 55 per cent while the wind would have picked up speed to 19.9 kilometres per hour, most usually from the south-east.

Spring

Spring is a delightful season, with the maximum temperature easing up from 24 degrees in September to 27 degrees in November. The minimum climbs too from 12 to 18 degrees. There are five to eight days of rain as the season progresses. The average wind conditions pick up after the winter lows, staring the season around 18 kilometres per hour and increasing to almost 20 kilometres per hour by the end.

Annual rainfall averages 1303 millimetres over the past 30 years, with the highest total of 2021 millimetres in 2010: the lowest was 832 millimetres in 2016. Overall, it is hard to beat the climate on Main Beach, its balmy subtropical weather encourages a relaxed attitude to life, occasionally disturbed by violent storms, but these usually pass through relatively quickly. We average 245 days of fine, sunny weather each year.

-

- o O o -

Our walk

Main Beach is an outdoorsy place. It is also a walkable place. The weather and the surroundings encourage you to walk to wherever you want to go locally.

The serenity of Hill Parade

We habitually head out in the afternoon walking west along the park-like tranquility of Hill Parade shaded by its majestic Norfolk Island pines and the calm of the eastern reach of the Nerang River, always providing their are no cowboys on jet-skis speeding by. These trees have a somewhat iconic status now on the Gold Coast. As our seaside settlements grew, it became the custom to plant Norfolk Island Pines and eventually they became part of the landscape. They are well suited to the coast because of their high tolerance to salt and wind. Ours on Hill Parade - which were planted about 30 years ago - are healthy and seem to enjoy life here, despite or maybe because of occasional battering from ferocious south-easters.

Along here we hope to get a sighting of our black swan family, who might be idling in the river or fossicking on the grass on the banks. We reach Tedder Avenue and the intersection with the Gold Coast Highway, turn left and are assailed by the traffic noise for about 150 metres or so as we walk beside it, before turning left into MacIntosh Island Park. The roar of the road noise quickly subsides and the park is tranquil. I am always struck just here by the majesty of the trees of various types and marvel that they must be younger than I am because where we now walk was just sand 40 years ago.

MacIntosh Island was originally a farm a hundred and more years ago. Old photos show it was initially well-treed, but was cleared around 1920 for the cultivation of small crops, such as passion fruit. In the 1960s, real estate developers' thoughts turned to building a resort on the island. It was split into two by the realigned Gold Coast Highway for the apartment blocks and houses that are now in Paradise Waters on the western section of the island. By the late 1970s and early 1980s, the eastern section was being designed and planted out as a park, and has grown into what it is now a cool oasis amongst the glitz, glamour and ceaseless traffic of the Gold Coast.

A couple of minutes later on our walk - we're heading more or less towards the ocean now - we look down on the small lake on our right that is sanctuary to "our" birds. Of course we do not own these birds but we do consider them acquaintances and they do so consider us, because they do not run or fly away when we approach. The most dominant are the flock of healthy white geese, perhaps half a dozen of them. There are other birds too. Usually around here you will see the flamboyant peacocks trying to catch the attention of the pea hens, who mostly seem to be unimpressed by the vivid display of those colourful tail feathers. There are white ibis pecking their way around and wading at the river's edge. There are too a few purple swamphens, with their brightly coloured dark-blue heads and purple chests.

On the other side of the path, to our left, we keep a watchful eye out for Bush Stone-Curlews in the undergrowth along the river bank. They are usually standing stock-still, sometimes sitting, and you can miss them because their camouflage is so good. Apparently they are more active at night, and we can occasionally hear their plaintiff nocturnal calls - a sort of "weer-loo" - from our apartment on the other side of the river. They are not quite as comfortable if you get too close, but nor are they a panicky lot.

We walk on past the playground, towards the small sandy beach on our left. Here we'll see a few seagulls paddling in the water, and here too is home for the Black Swans. At one stage

there was a black swan nest here that we reported on earlier. You may recall that the nesters - Mum and Dad - were chased away by the father of "our" swan family, and their dead eggs disposed of by council park staff.

A little further and we reach the pedestrian bridge across this reach of the Nerang River. We rarely see much wildlife from the bridge but are often disturbed by jet-skis, most of whose riders display no concern for the island, and indeed many actively disturb the river banks by fast swerving, sending splashing water onto the river banks and mangroves. This seems to be the game de jour.

We cross the bridge and Main Beach Parade to look out over the breaking waves of Narrowneck, and usually its surfers and wind surfers. This is a point of decision. Do we want to walk up the beach today? Is the tide in or out? If the sea isn't crashing into the back of the beach we usually do so. We pass a small enclosed enclave of rainforest, planted by the Gold Coast City Council, with a sign confidently declaring that "This rainforest has a future". It contains some relatively taller trees and bushes that provide cover for more delicate vines, orchids and ferns. We walk onto the beach at the Breaker Street Lifeguard Tower, and there before us stretches the wide Main Beach to the northern horizon, it seems, though in reality it is to the Spit seawall, perhaps four kilometres away.

Somewhere around here, usually a little further north, we see our resident flock of seagulls. They are always there, only their numbers vary. Sometimes there are a hundred or more, sometimes no more than a couple of dozen. There nearly always seems to be a couple taking off and flying somewhere out of sight, and two or three others returning from we know not where. There is occasional squabbling, but usually the gulls stand or sit quietly, minding their own business.

Further along the beach, towards the Southport Surf Life Saving Club our attention is drawn to the posh house next to the Woodroffe Avenue beach entrance to see whether its garden has suffered any further erosion, having been hit hard in a storm in 2022 that caused it to loose its front fence. The remaining steep sandy banks then became irresistible to children running up and sliding down them, causing further erosion. Nowadays a crude, hand-painted sign warns people to "KEEP OFF THE SAND DUNE".

Along the whole stretch of beach we keep an eye out for interesting shells. We note that there are sections where they are plentiful and then stretches were there are none, caused by variations in near shore sand formation and tides.

Beyond the Southport Surf Club we leave the human built environment behind. The high rise residential blocks fade from view and the beach is now fringed with she-oaks and sand hills capped with vines which prevent erosion. Along this stretch, we see only one or two seagulls, a very occasional pelican usually making it pretty obvious that he is hoping that a fisherman will share some bait. We do hear noisy rainbow parakeets in the trees. In the right time of the year - late May to September - we see an occasional whale breaching near the horizon, and very occasionally a mother whale and calf quite close in, not breaching, for it is too shallow, but swimming just on or below the surface, their presence given away by their blows they squirt out of their blowholes. Apparently mothers with calves often like to swim in close to shore and in shallow waters to better look after them.

You can walk all the way to the Spit Seawall, but we generally turn around not long after passing the patrolled beach at the Marina Mirage resort and head back to home.

Our walk always refreshes our minds and bodies. In fact I recently read of a study (one of quite a few) which found that we humans need at least two hours a week outside in nature to reap health benefits. A couple of hours of this, the U.K. university study said, is "associated with good health and wellbeing". Apparently it doesn't matter if you get the dose in one hit or on shorter spells spread over a week. And most nature visits in the study took place within just two kilometres of home.

And that is why paying attention to and enjoying the natural rhythms of Main Beach makes you feel so good.

- o O o -

About the Author

Rosey and John

John Tilston lives in Main Beach on the Gold Coast in Queensland Australia, close to the glorious golden sand beaches. For over 25 years he wrote for some of the world's most influential business publications. He was Melbourne Bureau Chief of the Australian Financial Review, Economics Editor for Business Day and London-based News Editor for Dow Jones Newswires. He has also contributed to Business Week, the Investors' Chronicle, the Financial Mail in Johannesburg, and The Sunday Times. He is the author of eight books. This is his first foray into writing about nature. He is married to the lovely Rosey.